45TH PARALLEL PRESS

Published in the United States of America by
Cherry Lake Publishing Group
Ann Arbor, Michigan
www.cherrylakepublishing.com

Reading Adviser: Beth Walker Gambro, MS, Ed., Reading Consultant, Yorkville, IL
Book Designer: Joseph Hatch

Photo Credits: MO NO/Pexels.com, cover; © Victoria Fox/Shutterstock, 4; cottonbro studio/Pexels.com, 7; Formerly attributed to George Gower, Public domain, via Wikimedia Commons, 8; © Featureflash Photo Agency/Shutterstock, 11; Public Doman, The Metropolitan Museum of Art, 13; © Livia Harijanto/Shutterstock, 14; Uncredited., Public domain, via Wikimedia Commons, 16; © New Africa/Shutterstock, 19; © FashionStock.com/Shutterstock, 21; SHVETS production/Pexels.com, 22; Nina zeynep güler ｡ zz/Pexels.com, 24; cottonbro studio/Pexels.com, 27; MART PRODUCTION/Pexels.com, 28; Stemaxc via Wikimedia Commons, 31

Copyright © 2026 by Cherry Lake Publishing Group

All rights reserved. No part of this book may be reproduced or utilized in any form or by any means without written permission from the publisher.

45th Parallel Press is an imprint of Cherry Lake Publishing Group.

Library of Congress Cataloging-in-Publication Data

Names: Loh-Hagan, Virginia author
Title: Cool clothes / written by Virginia Loh-Hagan.
Description: Ann Arbor, Michigan : 45th Parallel Press, [2025] | Series: Style it : trends and fads | Includes bibliographical references. | Audience: Grades 7-9 | Summary: "Clothes were cool way back when and they're still cool now! Take a look at the modern and historical trends and fads that have come and gone in the world of what to wear. Readers of these Hi-lo books will be surprised by various trends and fads that will keep them guessing until the very end"— Provided by publisher.
Identifiers: LCCN 2025008905 | ISBN 9781668963791 hardcover | ISBN 9781668965115 paperback | ISBN 9781668966723 ebook | ISBN 9781668968338 pdf
Subjects: LCSH: Fashion design—History—Juvenile literature | Exoticism in fashion—Juvenile literature
Classification: LCC TT507 .L727 2025 | DDC 746.9/2—dc23/eng/20250506
LC record available at https://lccn.loc.gov/2025008905

Cherry Lake Publishing Group would like to acknowledge the work of the Partnership for 21st Century Learning, a Network of Battelle for Kids. Please visit Battelle for Kids online for more information.

Note from publisher: Websites change regularly, and their future contents are outside of our control. Supervise children when conducting any recommended online searches for extended learning opportunities.

Printed in the United States of America

Dr. Virginia Loh-Hagan is an author and educator. She is currently the Executive Director for Asian American Native Hawaiian Pacific Islander Affairs at San Diego State University and the Co-Executive Director of The Asian American Education Project. She lives in San Diego with her very tall husband and very naughty dogs.

TABLe *of COnTenTs

INTRODUCTION **5**

CHAPTER 1: **Puffed Sleeves** **9**

CHAPTER 2: **Gaucho Pants** **10**

CHAPTER 3: **Poison Dresses** **12**

CHAPTER 4: **Killer Collars** **15**

CHAPTER 5: **Hobble Skirts**.................... **17**

CHAPTER 6: **Paper Dresses**.................... **18**

CHAPTER 7: **Logomania** **20**

CHAPTER 8: **Athleisure**......................... **23**

CHAPTER 9: **Frazzled English Woman** ... **25**

CHAPTER 10: **Dopamine Dressing**.......... **26**

DO YOUR PART! **29**
GLOSSARY **32**
LEARN MORE **32**
INDEX.. **32**

There are always new clothes trends! Which ones have you seen lately?

Introduction

Everybody has style. Some people have more style than others. They stand out. They use **fashion** to express themselves. Fashion is about how people want to look. It's about how people dress. It includes clothes, shoes, hats, and jewelry. It also includes hairstyles and makeup.

Fashion changes across cultures. It changes over time. There are many fashion **trends**. Trends are fads. They're patterns of change. They reflect what's popular at a certain time. Many people copy popular looks. They copy famous people. They get inspired. They want to be cool. They want to be in style.

Some trends last a long time. Other trends are short. All trends make history.

People wear clothes for different reasons. Most people have different outfits. There are outfits for work and school. There are outfits for working out. There are outfits for going out. There are outfits for staying in.

Clothes include dresses, pants, shirts, and jackets. People dress up their clothes. They add **accessories**. Accessories include belts, ties, purses, and scarves.

Clothes can change how people look. They can change how people feel. They show off people's personalities. They signal one's role in society. They play a key role in fashion.

Some clothes are fancy. Some are simple. Some are dangerous. (Remember, looks can kill!) There have been a lot of clothes trends. This book features some of the fun ones!

Jeans are a U.S. invention. They were invented in 1873. Today, everyone wears jeans.

Queen Elizabeth I of England made puffed sleeves even more popular.

CHAPTER  One

Puffed Sleeves

Puffed sleeves have been in style throughout history. Around the 1500s, **bombast** balloon sleeves were popular in Europe. Bombast was stuffing. It included materials such as cotton, wool, hair, or sawdust. It was heavy. It was uncomfortable. Bombast was added to sleeves. It made sleeves look puffy. Men also added bombast to have bigger bellies. Being big meant being wealthy and important.

In the 1800s, puffed sleeves became popular again. Instead of bombast, sleeve puffs were used. These puffs were like pillows filled with feathers. The bigger the better. Some women couldn't fit through doors.

In the 1980s, shoulder pads were in. They made shoulders look broader. Today, gently puffed sleeves are trendy.

Gaucho Pants

Gauchos are cowboys from Argentina and Uruguay. They had mixed European and Indigenous heritage. They herded cattle in the early 1800s. They lived off the land. They dressed for function. But their style became fashion.

They wore **bombachas**. These were baggy pants. They were ideal for long days of riding horses. They were comfortable. They were pleated at the waist. They had wide legs. They gathered at the ankles. They covered the tops of boots. Today, these pants are known as gaucho pants.

In the 1970s, gaucho pants became wide-legged pants for women. They ended around mid-calf. They were great options for pants that were like skirts.

FASHION-FORWARD PIONEER

Vera Wang is an Asian American designer. She worked for *Vogue*. *Vogue* is a fashion magazine. Wang was the youngest fashion editor at age 23. She left *Vogue*. She started designing. She's famous for her wedding gowns. Famous people wear her clothes. Wang made wedding gowns more modern. She gave women more options. She adapted to new trends. Her designs were classic and new. She said, "We showed women they didn't have to conform or dress a certain way." One of her collections was in red. In China, red means good fortune. Critics were shocked. Wang didn't care. She said, "You should be able to express yourself the way you want to."

Vera Wang in 2024

CHAPTER

Poison Dresses

Green was a hard color to make. A scientist learned that **arsenic** made a bright, strong green dye. Arsenic is a chemical element. It's used as poison.

Fabric was dyed with this arsenic green. This green fabric was made into dresses. These poison green dresses were popular in the 1870s. Women wore them. They got sick. Their stomachs ached. They couldn't see. They got skin rashes. But they wore these dresses only for special events. So they had limited contact. This saved their lives. Most didn't die.

But people who made the dresses were at risk. They touched the dyes all the time. They got blisters. They breathed in the poison. Many died.

This 1868 dress was likely dyed using arsenic green dye.

FASHION REBEL: TRENDSETTER

Jen Zeano celebrates Latina culture every day. Her wife is Veronica Zeano. Together, they own Jen Zeano Designs (JZD). They're based in Texas. Their first product was a pink "Latina Power" T-shirt. It was launched in 2016. It was a hit. Many of their designs feature inspiring words. They promote Latina pride. They promote gay pride. They were asked to design for Target stores. Their collection includes shirts, hats, jewelry, and more. Zeano said, "This collection was inspired by our journey to find our voices as Latinas in this country … the most important part of all of this is to continue to create pieces that allows our community to feel represented and reminds us all of the beauty of our cultura."

Killer Collars

Neckwear includes ties, scarves, and collars. European men wore high white collars. This was a sign of wealth. In the early 1900s, men's collars were **detachable**. This means they could be separated from the shirts. Men didn't have to change shirts when the collar got dirty.

Most of these collars were made from **starched** linen. Starched means to make stiff. This is done using a substance made from plants. Starching gave collars their shape. It held collars in place.

These collars weren't comfortable. They poked into necks and chins. They cut off blood supply. This caused men to faint. Some men choked. They couldn't breathe.

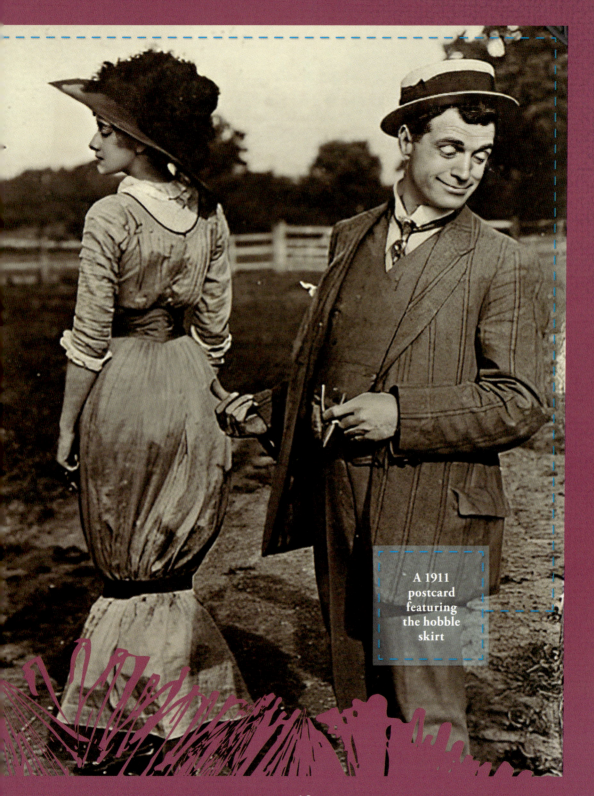

A 1911 postcard featuring the hobble skirt

CHAPTER

Hobble Skirts

Hobble skirts were tight. Hobble means to walk in an unsteady way. Hobble skirts were narrow. They used less fabric. But they restricted women's movement. They made women hobble. Hobble skirts were popular starting in 1908.

They were inspired by Japanese **kimonos**. A kimono is a robe. It's wrapped around the body. It's tied with a sash. Edith Ogilby Berg may have also inspired hobble skirts. Berg was the first U.S. woman to fly in a plane. A rope was tied around her ankles. This kept her skirt from blowing in the wind. Her look inspired a French designer.

Hobble skirts weren't safe. Some women died. They couldn't move out of danger. One woman tripped and fell off of a bridge. Women needed more freedom to move. They cut slits. They changed the design. The trend ended by 1914.

Paper Dresses

The Chinese invented paper in 105 CE. They made paper clothes. Japanese monks and peasants made paper clothes. In Europe, parts of outfits were made of paper.

But in the 1960s, paper dresses were a fashion hit. This happened in the United States and the United Kingdom. Clothing paper was stronger than regular paper. But these paper dresses still didn't last long. They could be worn about 3 times.

Many women loved them. Paper dresses were fun. They kept up with fast-changing trends. They were cheap. They were easy. No sewing was needed. Many could be made at once. This trend ended in the 1970s. People cared more about the environment. They didn't want to be wasteful.

DIY FASHION FUN

ADD YOUR OWN VIBE TO YOUR OUTFITS. CREATE YOUR OWN SPECIAL LOOK. HERE ARE SOME IDEAS:

» Upcycle used clothes. Sew on new designs. Cut up fabrics and create a new outfit. Make new products from old clothes. For example, use old jeans. Make dog beds or dog toys.

» Host a clothes swap to trade clothes with others. Freshen up your closet. Get new clothes without spending more money.

» Create yarn. Cut clothes or plastic bags into strips. Make a loom. Weave strips together. Make belts, scarves, and hats. Weaving is an ancient art. It is how fabrics are made.

CHAPTER seven

Logomania

Logos are company signs or symbols. Logomania started in the 1980s. It's the use of logos on clothing and other items. These logos are big. They're easy to see. Logomania signals status. People showed off brands.

Coco Chanel was the first to use her logo. Chanel is a French designer. In 1925, she put her initials on her designs. Initials are the first letters of words or names. Today's logos are bolder.

Dapper Dan is a Black American designer. He connected high fashion and hip-hop. He made logomania popular. He used logos in a new way. He took designer logos. He added them to his own designs. He reworked these pieces.

The Chanel name is clear on many of the brand's pieces.

Athleisure

Athleisure combines "**athletic**" and "**leisure**." Athletic means sporty. Leisure means free time. Athleisure is stylish activewear. It can be worn while working out. It can also be worn at work. It can be worn every day.

Athleisure includes yoga pants. It includes hoodies. It includes sports jackets. It also includes shoes. It's made from special fabrics. Fabrics are stretchy. They let air flow. They draw out sweat. Some even hide body odors.

Gym clothes have been around since the 1930s. But athleisure became a trend in the 2010s. It got more popular in 2020. It's still hot. It's popular with all ages. It promotes health and wellness.

> Many young people wear nothing but athleisure. It's their go-to style.

England isn't warm in the winter. That's why English women need to dress in layers and knitwear!

Frazzled English Woman

The "**Frazzled** English Woman" is a look. Frazzled means tired and nervous. This look was named in 2022. It was made popular on TikTok. But it started in the early 2000s. It was inspired by English characters in movies. These characters include Bridget Jones, Iris Simpkins, and others. These movies tend to be romantic comedies.

The style includes **layering**, knitwear, and a little chaos. Layering is wearing several pieces of clothing on top of each other. Knitwear includes sweaters and skinny scarves. The look also includes high boots, messy hair, and light makeup. It's stylish and messy at the same time.

CHAPTER

Dopamine Dressing

Dopamine is a chemical. It sends messages to the brain. It makes us feel good. Dopamine dressing started around 2022. It's dressing for joy. It's wearing clothes that make people feel strong and happy. It's all about feeling positive.

People wear bright colors. They wear bold patterns. They wear comfortable clothes. They wear different styles. They wear many accessories.

Dopamine dressing started after the 2020 lockdown. People didn't want to be practical. They didn't want to be trapped inside. They wanted to feel joy again. They wanted something new. They wanted more hope. They dressed to boost their moods.

Today, people are more intentional about what they wear.
They choose clothes that match their vibe. Clothes are personal.

Keep clothes made of plant materials, like cotton, in mind the next time you shop!

DO YOUR PART!

It's always fashionable to stand up for what's right. Fashion can be more than just about looks. It can be used to fight for causes. Be a fashion **activist**. Activists fight for change. They want a better world. Here are some ways to make a difference:

- Wear **cruelty-free**, **vegan** clothes. Cruelty-free means no animals were harmed. Vegan means no animals were used. Avoid leather. Avoid silk. Avoid fur and feathers.

- Instead, buy clothes made from plants. These materials include cotton, linen, and bamboo. Protect animals while still wearing great clothes.

- Wear the same clothes a lot. Avoid fast fashion. Fast fashion is a business model. Companies sell new clothes. They do this at low cost. Making clothes takes up a lot of energy and water. It adds chemicals to the air. It pollutes the air. This can be bad for nature. Save the planet.

- Research brands. Only buy from companies that support labor rights. Protect people.

- Respect cultures. People wear traditional clothes. They do this for cultural pride. Don't wear cultural clothes as costumes.

Remember, every little bit counts. Kindness matters. You can look good and feel great!

FIGHTING FOR JUSTICE

Aja Barber said, "You can love clothes and also love the planet."

She's a Black American woman. She's now living in England. She focuses on fashion and sustainability. Sustainability is the practice of using resources to support the future. Barber is part of the slow fashion movement. This movement supports well-paid labor. It supports good working conditions. It supports handmade pieces. It supports eco-friendly materials. It supports local shops. Barber focuses on style. She wants people to buy less. She said, "50% of what I buy is secondhand. But some of it is still new... 50% of my clothes are from ethical brands that I know and trust." She thinks people's shopping choices have power.

Glossary

accessories (ik-SEH-suh-reez) decorative or useful things worn in addition to clothing, such as purses, belts, ties, and scarves

activist (AAK-tih-vist) person who fights for political or social change

arsenic (AHRS-nik) poisonous chemical element that is mostly used to kill insects or weeds

athletic (ath-LEH-tik) relating to sports or fitness

bombachas (buhm-BAH-chuhz) loose, baggy pants gathered tightly at the ankle and worn especially in Argentina and Uruguay for riding and outdoor work

bombast (BAHM-bast) padding or stuffing made of materials such as cotton, wool, horsehair, and sawdust

cruelty-free (KROOL-tee-FREE) free from animal testing

detachable (dih-TACH-uh-buhl) able to be removed or separated from something

dopamine (DOH-puh-meen) a chemical messenger that is produced in the brain and is released when you do something enjoyable

fashion (FAA-shuhn) any way of dressing that is favored or popular at any one time or place

frazzled (FRA-zuhld) tired and nervous

gauchos (GOW-chohz) cowboys from Argentina and Uruguay in the early 1800s

hobble (HAH-buhl) to walk in an unsteady way

kimonos (kuh-MOH-nohs) long robe traditionally worn in Japan

layering (LAY-uhr-ing) wearing several pieces of clothing on top of each other

leisure (LEE-zhuhr) free time

logos (LOH-gohz) symbols or designs adopted by an organization to identify its products or brand

starched (STARCHD) using starch to make clothes stiff

trends (TRENDZ) fads or changes that are popular or common

vegan (VEE-guhn) containing no animal products

Learn More

Croll, Jennifer. *Bad Boys of Fashion: Style Rebels and Renegades Through the Ages.* Toronto, ON: Annick Press, 2019.

Hennessy, Kathryn, ed. *Fashion, New Edition: The Definitive Visual Guide.* New York, NY: DK, 2019.

Loh-Hagan, Virginia. *Fashion.* Ann Arbor, MI: Cherry Lake, 2021.

Millar, Christine Na-Eun. *History Is Worn: A Story of Fashion.* Los Angeles, CA: Honest History, 2023.

Index

accessories, 5–6, 21, 26–27
arsenic dye, 12–13
athleisure, 22–23

Barber, Aja, 31
Berg, Edith Ogilby, 17
bombachas, 10
bombast sleeves, 8–9

Chanel, Coco, 20–21
collars, 8, 15
cruelty-free clothing, 28–29, 31

Dapper Dan, 20
DIY projects, 19
dopamine dressing, 26–27
dresses, 6, 8, 12–13, 18

Elizabeth I, 8
ethical clothing, 18–19, 28–31

fashion designers, 11, 14, 20
fast and slow fashion, 30–31
"Frazzled English Woman" look, 24–25

gaucho pants, 10

hobble skirts, 16–17

jeans, 6–7, 19

kimonos, 17
knitwear, 19, 24–25

layering, 24–25
logos, 20–21
luxury brands, 20–21

neckwear, 6, 15

pants, 6–7, 10, 22–23
puffed sleeves, 8–9

skirts, 16–17
sportswear, 22–23
sustainability, 18–19, 28–31

upcycled clothing, 19, 31

vegan clothing, 28–29, 31

Wang, Vera, 11
weaving, 19

Zeano, Jen, 14